Holiday Express

A Visit to the Holiday Train Show at

THE NEW YORK BOTANICAL GARDEN

PHOTOGRAPHS BY JOHN PEDEN

Fifteen years have sped by since we introduced the *Holiday Train Show* at The New York Botanical Garden. The show has developed and expanded in a myriad of delightful ways—more trains and tracks, even overhead; new landmark buildings; ever more creative landscapes— to name just a few, courtesy of the designer Paul Busse and Garden curator Francisca Coelho.

The *Holiday Train Show* is set within the curving, elegant glasshouse galleries of the Enid A. Haupt Conservatory. Lit by the winter sky dwarf conifers and hollies, winter-flowering cyclamen, Christmas cactus, African violets, and other charming diminutive flowers add to the enchantment of this beloved Garden show.

Across these pages, and in the show itself, you will tour the majestic Hudson Valley, with its landmarks marvelously replicated in bark, twig, seed, berry, and other natural materials found in the plant kingdom. Travel from elegant mansions upriver, including Olana and Kykuit, through the Bronx to Yankee Stadium, down to Manhattan and its architectural icons—among them the Empire State Building, the Guggenheim Museum, Rockefeller Center, and the Statue of Liberty with a gown of palm fronds.

For many years, this holiday tradition has been a gift to the people of New York from Victoria and Robert Zoellner and their family. Millions of children and their parents have had their spirits lifted by a holiday visit to the Botanical Garden since the show began. In recent years the Zoellners have been joined by Pfizer. We extend our heartiest thanks to these generous gift givers.

Gregory Long

Gregory Long, *President*
The New York Botanical Garden

5

Dear Friends:

It is with great pleasure that we have been associated with the *Holiday Train Show* almost from the very beginning. We love the Botanical Garden and the holiday season, and are thrilled that this annual event has become such a cherished tradition for tens of thousands of New Yorkers. Bringing grandparents and grandkids, toddlers and their parents, friends and strangers together during the holiday season is a delight indeed. Everyone who comes is mesmerized by New York landmarks masterfully recreated from plant parts, by trains racing from gallery to gallery and soaring overhead, and by plants from the tropics and the deserts all beautifully curated in one of the most spectacular settings in the world. How lucky we are to help people discover this!

May all good things be yours during this holiday season.

Victoria and Robert Zoellner

To visit the *Holiday Train Show* in the Enid A. Haupt Conservatory at The New York Botanical Garden is to enter another world—a world of pure enchantment on so many levels.

Expectations are heightened by the season, which sets the stage with an undercurrent of anticipation: music, lights, parties, families reuniting, snow—or at least wintry weather—gifts, and a thousand different holiday traditions. At the *Holiday Train Show*, anticipation starts with snowflake lights sparkling overhead and a resplendent Christmas tree at the entrance to the Conservatory. Once inside the doors, the air is briefly balmy as one traverses the various tropical houses of the Conservatory en route to the show. And then, there it is.

For the littlest ones, there's the thrill of seeing trains, trains, and more trains, all an understandable size, rolling along track everywhere they look, in a diminutive landscape that offers excitement of its own: waterfalls, tunnels, forests of glittering evergreens. Some of the train track does amazing things. It disappears around a bend and reappears high overhead crossing a bridge, only to disappear again and emerge behind a building, which magically is one's own size and made of bark, twigs, and leaves!

For those of us who have left the age of such innocent wonderment behind, there's the undeniable delight of seeing a meticulously created landscape within a splendid Victorian glasshouse. But that's just the beginning. Looking closer, we see sophisticated replicas of New York buildings all made from dried plant materials. Brick façades built with tiny pieces of bark,

9

siding assembled from reeds, roofing composed of moss, 20-foot bridge spans made with branches, tunnels of hollowed log. And then there are the details: the Statue of Liberty in a robe of palm fronds and grasses holding high a pomegranate torch with a flame of dried monarch flower; the spirals of Frank Lloyd Wright's Guggenheim Museum echoed with black locust shelf fungi in our botanical version; the marquee of Radio City Music Hall reproduced in radish and catalpa seeds.

Some of the structures are familiar landmarks, others less well known or no longer standing. Working from photographs, show creator Paul Busse and his crew create easily recognizable, small-scale translations rather than precise replicas. Just as a skilled caricaturist captures a personality with a few strokes of a pen, they capture the essential, distinguishing elements of a building with plant materials. Berries, seeds, pods, and vines add texture and detail, and, of course, are the key to making the whole design harmonious in a garden setting.

The *Holiday Train Show* combines the designer's love of trains with a landscape architect's eye for detail and an artisan's imaginative use of plants. The New York Botanical Garden and Paul began their collaboration in 1992, and every year thereafter the show has become more elaborate. It takes a crew of close to 20 about 10 days to lay out the 1,200 feet of track, get the trains running, construct the trestles, position the buildings, tuck in the hundreds of plants, and place the lights just so. The track arrangement consists of simple loops, with the tracks woven into the landscape and screened by houses and plants. With as many as 11 trains running at any time, there is always that delightful feeling of anticipation, waiting for a train to reappear.

Together with the venue of the grand Conservatory, the show makes for a delightful holiday experience. Indeed, it has become one of New York City's most beloved traditions, or as the *New York Times* puts it, "one of New York City's best holiday gifts to itself."

About the Trains

The trains in The New York Botanical Garden *Holiday Train Show* are G-gauge trains. Designed to be run outdoors, they have motors and gears that are housed in weatherproof casings. They are powered

with low voltage on gauge-1 brass track, which measures 1 ¾ inches (45 mm) between the rails. A large-scale steam locomotive can measure over 2 feet long and weigh as much as 10 pounds.

The locomotives and railroad cars in the *Holiday Train Show* represent American trains from late 1800s steam engines to today's most modern high-speed passenger trains. Model trains, however, have existed since the inception of the railroad industry in the 1830s. Many of the earliest models were built for competitions sponsored by railroads to encourage inventors to solve early engineering problems. Others were built to gain the public's interest or to entice financial backers to support new railway lines. Afterward, these steam models—some of which were large enough to ride on—were often given to the investors' children and installed outdoors on spacious estates.

Soon toy manufacturers started making model trains. But just as in the world of full-size trains, there was no consistency in the gauge of the track or the scale of the trains. This problem was solved in the 1880s when the German company Märklin established standardized gauges and scales. Before long, almost all

American and European model manufacturers had adopted these standards. Most of these railroads were still built for use outdoors and eventually the term "garden railway" came to be used to describe model railroads which, with suitable landscaping, became decorative and entertaining features in the garden.

In 1967 the German firm of Ernst Paul Lehmann introduced Lehmann's Gross Bahn (LGB), or Lehmann's Big Trains, made of modern UV-resistant plastic and modeled on German narrow-gauge trains. They were sturdy and designed to run outdoors on standard gauge-1 track. These new LGBs were not immediately popular in the United States as there were no models of American trains. However, in 1985 LGB introduced a model of a Colorado narrow-gauge steam engine, the *Mogul*. American narrow-gauge railroads were designed as short-line systems where the terrain was too steep for standard railroads. With models of American trains now available, garden railroading as a hobby became popular in the United States. Nowadays, many U.S. manufacturers make large-scale trains—among them Aristo-Craft, Bachmann, Lionel, and USA Trains.

About The New York Botanical Garden

Nathaniel Lord Britton, an eminent Columbia University botanist, and his wife, Elizabeth, also a botanist, were so inspired by their 1888 visit to the Royal Botanic Gardens, Kew, near London, that they decided that New York should possess a great botanical garden. A magnificent site was selected in the northern section of the Bronx, part of which had belonged to the vast estate of tobacco merchant Pierre Lorillard. In 1891 the land was set aside by the State Legislature for the creation of "a public botanic garden of the highest class" for the City of New York. Prominent civic leaders and financiers, including Andrew Carnegie, Cornelius Vanderbilt II, and J. Pierpont Morgan, agreed to match the City's commitment to finance the buildings and improvements, initiating a public-private partnership that continues today.

Now in its second century, the Botanical Garden is one of the world's great collections of plants, the region's leading educational center for gardening and horticulture, and an international center for botanical research. The Garden is alive with opportunities for discovery, from an ecotour of the world in the Enid A. Haupt Conservatory to an innovative indoor/outdoor hands-on science museum for children to 50 exquisite gardens and plant collections, all on a 250-acre National Historic Landmark site that includes 50 acres of the native Forest that once covered New York City.

In addition to the beauty of its natural topography, the scope of its plant collections, and the distinction of its designed gardens and curatorial excellence, the Botanical Garden is celebrated for the ambitious goals of its scientific research and educational programs as well as its careful stewardship of this unique site. The Garden is not just an urban greensward, open-air classroom, major arboretum, or delightful array of display gardens; nor is it simply a place of respite and scholarship. It is all of these things combined.

Little Red Lighthouse
(1880)
Below the George Washington Bridge, Manhattan

The Little Red Lighthouse, originally built in 1880 for Sandy Hook, New Jersey, was moved to its present location in 1921. Hildegarde H. Swift and Lynd Ward immortalized it in a 1942 children's book, *The Little Red Lighthouse and the Great Gray Bridge*. After navigational lights were installed on the bridge, the lighthouse was put up for auction. The outcry from a barrage of letters from children who loved the book saved the lighthouse, and it is still maintained by the City of New York. Our model has siding of tinted magnolia leaves and a lotus seed pod for the peaked roof. The "light" in the windows is white birch bark.

St. Patrick's Cathedral

Saks Fifth Avenue

Metropolitan Life Insurance Tower

Chrysler

Rockefeller Center

Flatiron Building   Grand Central Terminal

City Music Hall

Saks Fifth Avenue (1924)

611 Fifth Avenue, Manhattan
Architects Starrett & Van Vleck designed this luxurious emporium in 1922 in a Renaissance-inspired style appropriate to the exclusive character of Fifth Avenue. Our version has balcony rails and posts made of Virginia creeper and screwbean mesquite. The pillars on the fourth floor between the windows are made with sugar pine cone scales, yew bark, and acorn caps. Top floor railings are sugar pine cone scales, eucalyptus pods, and bittersweet vines, while the cornice is crowned with willow, Russian sage, and white pine cone scales. The doors have juniper berry handles.

Metropolitan Life Insurance Tower (1909)

1 Madison Avenue, Manhattan
Designed by Napoleon LeBrun & Sons, the campanile-style tower of the Metropolitan Life Insurance Company with its slender shaft, enormous roof, and cupola evokes the famed bell tower of San Marco in Venice. For a time this was the tallest building in the world. Our replica is crafted from honeysuckle, pine cones, corkscrew hazel, and bamboo.

Rockefeller Center (1932–1940)

48th to 51st Streets between
Fifth and Sixth Avenues, Manhattan
The Art Deco centerpiece of Rockefeller Center, the RCA Building (now the GE Building), was designed by Raymond Hood. It overlooks the shops, restaurants, and, in winter, the outdoor skating rink of Rockefeller Plaza, all presided over by a gilded bronze sculpture of Prometheus by Paul Manship. Our Prometheus is composed of tree fungus, eucalyptus leaves, gravevine, acorn caps, moss, and metal leaf. Our building is made with Norway maple and hickory barks and decorated with sugar pine cone scales, lemon leaves, nigella pods, rose hips eucalyptus leaves, and maple seeds. The angels in the Channel Gardens are made with okra pods, grapevine, hickory nuts, sea grass, and raffia.

15

St. Patrick's Cathedral

Previous spread

Chrysler Building (1930)

405 Lexington Avenue, Manhattan

This Art Deco crown jewel of the New York skyline was also, for a few months, the tallest building in the world until the completion of the Empire State Building. It juxtaposes linear curves with sharp angles. Our version has a ginkgo leaf surface with corkscrew hazel branches making up the contoured areas. Sugar pine cone scales form the roof, with small gourds projecting from the corners representing the building's eight stainless steel, eagle-like gargoyles. The spire is a honey locust thorn.

Radio City Music Hall (1932)

1260 Sixth Avenue, Manhattan

An important example of Art Deco architecture, Radio City was designed by Edward Durrell Stone, who later created the original Museum of Modern Art. When it opened in 1932, Radio City was the nation's largest theater. The marquee, a full city block long, is reproduced here with willow, pear-shaped pods, and tinted radish and catalpa seeds. The façade is maple bark with doors of red twig dogwood and grapevine twines. The window frames are dyed lemon branches, and dyed lemon leaves appear between the windows to recreate the Art Deco detail.

Flatiron Building (1903)

175 Fifth Avenue, Manhattan

This unusual building, designed by Daniel H. Burnham, marks the beginning of the skyscraper era in New York City. The triangular shape is the result of Broadway's diagonal route through Manhattan's street grid. The rounded apex at 23rd Street measures only 6 feet across. The rounded corners of our version are made of white pine cones, lotus pods, and dried beans. Lemon and oak leaves are used for horizontal ornamentation, and the spire is a pomegranate with a honey locust thorn.

St. Patrick's Cathedral (1858–1888)

Fifth Avenue between 50th and 51st Streets, Manhattan

A glorious structure by James Renwick, Jr., and William Rodrigue, St. Patrick's is the largest Gothic-style Roman Catholic cathedral in the United States. The Catholic Church bought the land in 1828 intending to use it as a cemetery, but abandoned the plan when gravediggers hit rock just below the surface. Work on the Cathedral began in 1858, but was suspended during the Civil War; it was finally completed in 1888. In our version, intricately carved granite is cleverly replicated with dozens of different plants, including eucalyptus leaves and pods, pepperberries, Siberian iris seed pods, and gourds.

Grand Central Terminal (1903–1913)

42nd Street and Park Avenue, Manhattan

This Beaux Arts-style station embodies the romance and glamour of the Golden Age of Rail and remains a civic design triumph of architecture, technology, and city planning. The building is topped by a 1,500-ton sculpture of Mercury, Hercules, Minerva, and an eagle, symbolizing commerce on the move, sustained by moral and mental energy. Our rooftop sculpture is crafted from dried strawflowers, arborvitae, and yarrow. The façade is made of sand and blocks of sycamore bark, roofed with southern magnolia leaves. The lampposts are fashioned from honeysuckle stems and acorns.

South Street Seaport Historic District

Statue of Liberty

South Street Seaport Historic District (ca. 1793–1811)

Fulton and South Streets, Manhattan

The warehouses and counting houses of South Street Seaport were built by Peter Schermerhorn, a merchant and ship owner, when the area was New York's major shipping center. The corner building is made of lobed oak leaf, cinnamon sticks, walnut shells, bark, and honeysuckle. Sliced branches are used for the sign. The other buildings are made of eucalyptus seed pods and magnolia leaves, honeysuckle, cinnamon sticks, and a pine cone roof.

United Nations Headquarters (1947–1953)

United Nations Plaza, Manhattan

The U.N. complex consists of four buildings on 18 acres along the East River: the 39-story Secretariat building, General Assembly, Library and Conference Building. An appropriately international team of architects, led by Wallace K. Harrison and Le Corbusier, was assembled to design it. Our façade is made of sand and colored tile grout. The national flags are a variety of different leaves.

Statue of Liberty (1871–1886)

Liberty Island, New York Harbor

A gift from the French to commemorate the centennial of the Declaration of Independence, the statue was designed by Fréderic-Auguste Bartholdi and shipped to America in 350 pieces. The pedestal was designed by Richard Morris Hunt and paid for with private donations. From the ground to the tip of her torch the statue measures 305 feet. Our Lady Liberty's robes are made from palm fronds and grasses, her necklace from stalks of wheat, and her torch flame from a dried monarch flower inside a pomegranate half.

City Hall (1812)

City Hall Park between Broadway and Park Row, Manhattan

The design for City Hall was conceived of as a grand combination of Federal style with French Renaissance detail by Joseph François Mangin, a French architect who worked on the Place de la Concorde in Paris, and John McComb, Jr., a well-known New York City architect. Its original façade, fabricated with soft Massachusetts marble, eroded badly and was replaced with Alabama limestone. Our replica is fashioned from hickory, elm, and maple bark with Virginia creeper, honeysuckle twigs, pine cone scales, dusty miller leaves, okra seeds, acorn tops, and corkscrew hazel. The statue of Justice is made with palm and tobacco leaves, cattail stems, raffia, wheat, and butternut hickory. The flagpoles are formed from red twig dogwood with bittersweet vines, acorns, and honey locust pods.

Tammany Hall (1867)

14th Street, Manhattan

Formed in 1789, The New York Tammany Society was named after Tamanend, Indian chief of the Delawares. Originally a patriotic and charitable organization, it soon became a political force that lasted for well over a century, eventually becoming synonymous with political corruption. The Society's third home on 14th Street east of Broadway, topped by a statue of Chief Tamanend, was demolished to make way for a Con Ed office building in 1929. Our Chief is made of oak leaves, reeds, grapevine, and corkscrew hazel. The building's ornament consists of willow twigs, acorn caps, and reeds. Its façade is made of sand and grout.

Public Baths (1906)

East 23rd Street and Asser Levy Place, Manhattan

Designed by William Martin Aiken and Arnold Brunner, this elegant Beaux-Arts building, modeled after the baths of ancient Rome, housed public baths that encompassed a full block. Twin low arches flanked by Doric columns separate men's and women's entries. The doors on our entryways are made of bark with pine cone scales and topped by cinnamon stick, canella berry, and star-anise pediments. Moneta leaves form the façade. The roof ornament features poppy seed and eucalyptus pods, acorn caps, and hemlock cones.

Solomon R. Guggenheim Museum

Washington Arch

Queens Insurance Company   Mrs. George T. Bliss House   93 Reade Street

93 Reade Street

Previous spread

Washington Arch (1889–1895)

Washington Square Park, Manhattan

Standing at the entrance to Washington Square Park is the Washington Arch, designed by McKim, Mead & White. In the aftermath of the Revolutionary War, the park was used as a potter's field and dueling ground. In the 1820s, the elite of New York began building elegant town houses around the park, which served as the nucleus of New York's old society, written about so poignantly by Henry James in *Washington Square* (1881). Our arch is crafted of willow, canella berries, walnut shells, and pine bark.

Queens Insurance Company (1877)

37–39 Wall Street, Manhattan

This red brick and stone structure, now destroyed, was designed in a Venetian-influenced late Romanesque/Early Gothic style. It was distinguished by its overscaled stoop and entrance portico and by the expansive glazed arch storefront at street level. Our storefront windows are configured from two different kinds of bark, while the sand in tinted grout façade is decorated with bark, twigs, canella seeds, and star-anise.

Mrs. George T. Bliss House (1907)

9 East 68th Street, Manhattan

Architecturally, this elegant house is similar in spirit to that of the famous British Regency architect, Sir John Soane. The Metropolitan Museum of Art possesses a large stained glass window from the house of a classically garbed allegory of Welcome modeled on Mrs. Bliss's daughter by John La Farge. Our version's façade is sand in tinted grout with birch branches for the half columns. The column bases and lintels are made of bark strips. Grapevine tendrils and eucalyptus pods are used for ornamentation.

93 Reade Street (1857)

Manhattan

This elegant, Italianate, cast-iron front building has scarcely less glass than today's skyscrapers. It was designed and made by one of New York's most successful 19th-century iron foundries, Daniel Badger's Architectural Iron Works. Its fluted Corinthian columns diminish in height from floor to floor and are gracefully topped by an elaborate cornice. Our building's front is adorned with catkins, pine cone scales, acorn caps, and canella berries.

Solomon R. Guggenheim Museum (1956–1959)

1071 Fifth Avenue, Manhattan

Frank Lloyd Wright's only design in New York City, the Guggenheim Museum is one of the city's most unique and controversial buildings. A symphony of triangles, ovals, arcs, circles, and squares, its central spiral form recalls a nautilus shell with continuous spaces flowing freely into one another. The modern and contemporary art is displayed on the walls of a ramp in the center of the spiral that gradually rises to 92 feet, with additional galleries extending from it. Our version is fabricated from black locust shelf fungi, birch twigs, and acorn caps.

The Jewish Museum (1909)

1109 Fifth Avenue, Manhattan

Charles Pierrepont Henry Gilbert, a prominent New York
architect of the late 19th and early 20th centuries, designed
this building as a private home for the family of Felix
Warburg. Gilbert's specialty was designing grand, chateau-
style houses on Fifth Avenue for wealthy New York patrons
like investment bankers Warburg and Otto Kahn and
entrepreneur Frank Woolworth. In 1944, the Warburg family
donated the home to The Jewish Museum, which opened
in 1947. Our museum has a façade of sand in tinted grout,
windows of willow, wheat stems, rose hips, corkscrew hazel,
and maple bark topped by juniper berries, pine, hemlock,
and spruce cones. The columns are winged euonymus,
acorns, spruce cones, lotus pods, and wheat.

Angel of the Waters

34

Angel of the Waters (1873)
Bethesda Fountain, Central Park, Manhattan
Angel of the Waters is the graceful sculpture that tops Bethesda Fountain in Central Park. The lily in her hand represents Purity, while the four figures below represent Peace, Health, Purity, and Temperance. Designer Emma Stebbins, the first woman to receive a sculptural commission in New York City, likened the healing powers of the angel to that of the clean and pure Croton Reservoir water. Our replica is composed of orange slices, pear-shaped pods, lemon leaves, eucalyptus leaves, sugar pine cone scales, hemlock cones, and wisteria pods.

Frick Collection (1914)
1 East 70th Street, Manhattan
Designed by Carrère & Hastings, this Louis XV-style mansion was built at enormous cost by Henry Clay Frick as both his residence and a home for his art collection. The design reflects his plan to leave both to the public. The Frick Collection includes over a thousand works of art from the Renaissance to the late 19th century. Corkscrew hazel, gourds and leaves were used to create our mansion. Sweetgum seed capsules, eucalyptus pods, grapevine tendrils, pine cone scales, and acorn caps form the railing.

Willard Straight House (1915)

1130 Fifth Avenue, Manhattan
This handsome neo-Georgian house at the corner of Fifth
Avenue and 94th Street was designed by Delano & Aldrich,
a firm responsible for many handsome New York buildings of
the period. Straight was a businessman, diplomat, and founder,
with his wife, of several magazines, including *The New Republic*.
Eventually the house became the headquarters of the Audubon
Society and then the International Center for Photography.
Our Straight House is made of sycamore bark, acorn caps,
screwbean mesquite pods, oak leaves, and honeysuckle sticks.

Philip and Maria Kleeberg House (1898)

3 Riverside Drive, Manhattan
Charles P.H. Gilbert designed the Kleeberg house among many
other mansions for New York's elite. Trained at the Ecole des
Beaux-Arts in Paris, he was known for his chateau-style houses,
but he dabbled in many different styles, this house being a freely
interpreted Dutch Renaissance concoction. According to his
granddaughter, his employees claimed the initials P.H. stood for
"Particular as Hell." Our replica is decorated with hemlock cones,
leaves, pine cone scales, acorn caps, pine bark nuggets, cattails,
and grape vine. The roof is made of eucalyptus twigs and seeds.

Willard Straight House

Willard Straight House

Edith and Ernesto G. Fabbri House

Theodore Roosevelt Birthplace

Scheffel Hall

Philip and Maria Kleeberg House

Collectors' Club

David S. Brown Store

Edith and Ernesto G. Fabbri House   Scheffel Hall   Collectors' Club

Theodore Roosevelt Birthplace (1848)

28 East 20th Street, Manhattan

The original building, where the 26th President of the United States was born and lived until he was 14, was demolished in 1916. After Roosevelt's death, the site was purchased by the Women's Roosevelt Memorial Association and the house was reconstructed in 1923 by one of the nation's first successful woman architects, the aptly named (for this project, at least) Theodate Pope Riddle. Our version has a façade of bark squares with honeysuckle twig and dried moss details.

David S. Brown Store (1876)

8 Thomas Street, Manhattan

David S. Brown & Co. soap manufacturers commissioned Morgan Slade to design this whimsical structure. A favorite among architecture aficionados, it successfully incorporates many styles, including Venetian Gothic and Romanesque. Our reproduction uses tinted lemon leaves for the window arches, dried pomegranate for the roof over the door, and seagrass rope for columns. Magnolia leaves, pine cones, dried orange slices, corkscrew willow, cinnamon stick slices, juniper berries, whole peppercorns, red twig dogwood, and oak bark are used for ornamentation.

Edith and Ernesto G. Fabbri House (1900)

11 East 62nd Street, Manhattan

Continuing the Vanderbilt family tradition of building houses for their children (and what houses they were!), William H. Vanderbilt's daughter Margaret built this beautiful Beaux-Arts building for her daughter and son-in-law, Edith and Ernesto Fabbri. It is now the residence of the permanent representative of Japan to the United Nations. Our version is fashioned from pear-shaped pods, maple leaves, wisteria pods, orange slices, screwbean mesquite pods, rice flowers, sugar pine cone scales, acorn caps, and eucalyptus pods.

Scheffel Hall (1894)

190 Third Avenue, Manhattan

A beer hall that catered to the large German population around East 14th Street in the 19th century, this exuberant German Renaissance building with its scrolled gable is actually an 1894 façade placed on an older building. The hall was named for Joseph Victor von Scheffel, a German balladeer known for his songs about fellowship and love. Our Hall has siding of moneta leaves, windows of willow, red twig dogwood, pine cone scales, screwbean mesquite pods, and cinnamon sticks and roof ornamentation made with walnut shells, eucalyptus pods, poppy pods and tops, and hemlock cones.

Collectors' Club (1902)

22 East 35th Street, Manhattan

Founded in 1896, the Collectors' Club is one of America's premier philatelic organizations. Its home, an elegant neo-Georgian, five-story brownstone in Manhattan, was completely redesigned by McKim, Mead & White in 1902. Alfred Lichtenstein, one of the giants of early philately, donated it to the Club in 1938. With columns and portals along the front, this likeness is composed of broom and willow sticks, corkscrew hazel pieces, red-tinted magnolia leaves, grapevine, and acorn caps.

Edith and Ernesto G. Fabbri House

39

New Amsterdam Theater

New Amsterdam Theater (1903)

214 West 42nd Street, Manhattan
This highly decorative, dramatic building helped
turn Times Square into a glittering and festive
theater district and is one of the oldest surviving
legitimate theaters on Broadway. The design by
Herts & Tallant combined Art Nouveau style with
Germanic medievalism and classicism. The theater
was bought by The Walt Disney Company in the
1990s and beautifully restored. Our little theater
is adorned with pepperberries, eucalyptus pods,
cinnamon slices, acorn caps, pine cones, orange
slices, bittersweet berries, and pear-shaped pods.

Aguilar Library (1899)

174 East 110th Street, Manhattan
Our model recreates the original building designed
by Herts & Tallant, which was expanded and had a
new façade added in 1905. The library, founded in
1886 as an independent library to serve immigrant
Jews, was named after Grace Aguilar, an English
novelist of Sephardic descent. It is now part of the
New York Public Library system. The stone work on
our replica is made of bark squares. The balcony is
formed with pear-shaped pods and corkscrew hazel.

New Amsterdam Theater

Nathan Straus House

wn House

Lanier House

Brooklyn Brownstone

Squad Company 41

Brownstone

Nathan Straus House

Previous spread

Brooklyn Brownstone (ca. 1870)

Brownstone is a soft, close-grained sandstone. Available locally, it was an inexpensive alternative to marble and limestone and quickly became popular in the mid-1800s for everything from Fifth Avenue mansions to humble rowhouses. Indeed, it was so popular that the term became common for any rowhouse. A true brownstone, however, is an ordinary brick rowhouse with a brownstone front and a front stoop. Our front is sand in tinted grout with bark and grapevine tendril ornamentation. The roof is fashioned from pine cone scales.

Town House (ca. 1890)

5 East 68th Street, Manhattan

Originally the term "town house" was used to distinguish a city residence from a country house of the same owner. It is now generally used to describe a home in an urban configuration, such as a rowhouse. "Town house," however, sounding more elegant, is generally better for sales. Some of New York's 19th- and early 20th-century town houses were very elegant indeed. Our town house's façade is sand in grout with bark squares. The front door and window ornaments are made of cedrela seed pods, cinnamon stick slices, and star-anise.

J.F.D. Lanier House (1903)

123 East 35th Street, Manhattan

Financier James Franklin Doughty Lanier and his wife, Harriet, hired the architectural firm of Hoppin & Koen, whose partners had both worked at McKim, Mead & White, to design their handsome Beaux-Arts town house. Lanier had moved to New York from Indiana, which remained dear to his heart. Twice he loaned the state what amounted to over a million dollars without any security. Both times he was repaid. Our replica is elegantly decorated with eucalyptus and cedrela seed pods, catkins, and honeysuckle twigs.

Nathan Straus House (1896)

27 West 72nd Street, Manhattan

After Nathan Straus made his fortune as a partner of the New York department stores Abraham and Straus and R. H. Macy and Co., he turned to philanthropy. He advocated milk pasteurization as a means to check the spread of tuberculosis and provided relief for the poor during economic and natural disasters. He also served as Park Commissioner and as President of the Board of Health. Our version of his house has a stoop made of moneta leaves and willow twigs; windows adorned with cinnamon sticks, nigella pods, acorn caps, and canella berries and a balcony made of red twig dogwood and screwbean mesquite pods.

Squad Company 41 (1903)

330 East 150th Street, Bronx

This three-story, Beaux Arts-style building is one of several firehouses designed by Alexander Stevens, the Fire Department's Superintendent of Buildings in the early 20th century. The ornate structure houses Squad Company 41, which serves battalions in both the Bronx and Upper Manhattan. Originally called Engine 41, the company moved into these headquarters on April 4, 1904. Birch, hickory, and osage orange barks were used to create our firehouse, along with pear-shaped pods, poppy pods, willow twigs, cinnamon sticks, sea grass cord, and fern leaves.

Brownstone   Squad Company 41

Yankee Stadium (1923)

Bronx

In 1921, the New York Yankees purchased 10 acres of property in the Bronx to build a new ballpark. The stadium, completed in just 284 days, was ready for the inaugural game on April 18, 1923 against the Boston Red Sox. Because legendary slugger Babe Ruth's drawing power helped make the new structure possible, it became known as "The House that Ruth Built." The classic original stadium, which underwent later redesigns and renovations, is memorialized in our replica.

The outside wall is made of horse chestnut bark, the seats of elm bark, and the field walls of cherry bark. The pillars are willow sticks, the light towers are willow twigs and acorn tops, and the top detailing is a combination of cinnamon sticks, burning bush twigs, acorn tops, and willow.

Queens County Farm (1772)

73-50 Little Neck Parkway, Queens

The Dutch-style farmhouse was built in 1772 by Jacob Adriance on land purchased by his grandfather, Elbert, in 1697. It doubled in size in the 1830s and remained a working farm until 1960. In 1975 it became the Queens County Farm Museum, the only working historical farm in New York City. Our farmhouse has maple leaf siding, dried moss for roofing, and decorative touches from honeysuckle vine and pepperberries.

Bowne House (1661)

37-01 Bowne Street, Queens

Still occupying its original site, Bowne House represents a blend of the two main architectural traditions of colonial New York with a Dutch design and English building techniques. The last alterations were made in the early 19th century. The house was built by John Bowne, a Quaker, and it was the first indoor meeting place of the forbidden Society of Friends. The Bowne House Historical Society was founded in 1946, and the house has operated as a museum since 1947. Our version has an oak leaf roof with dried moss and grapevine tendril touches.

King Manor (1730–1806)

Jamaica Avenue, Queens

Rufus King was an important figure in early U.S. history and a lifelong opponent of slavery. A delegate to the Constitutional Convention in 1787, he then became a senator from New York. He was also ambassador to Great Britain and ran for President against James Monroe in 1816. The oldest house in Jamaica, Queens, King purchased the 11 acres of land and its buildings for $12,000 in 1805. After his death the estate went to his son, John Alsop King, who became Governor of New York. The walls of our manor are made of white birch bark, the shutters of redbud seed pods, and the roof of wheat.

Dyckman House (1785)

4881 Broadway and West 204th Street, Manhattan

A typical 18th-century, Dutch colonial farmhouse, Dyckman House is the last of its kind in Manhattan. During the Revolution, the Continental Army, retreating from Harlem Heights, occupied the original farmhouse. Subsequently the British used it during their occupation of Manhattan. When the British withdrew in 1783, they burned it, but it was rebuilt by William Dyckman. The farm eventually grew to 400 acres, making it the largest in Manhattan. Our house has a dried arborvitae roof, and birch and cherry twigs form the porch columns and railing.

Lyndhurst (1865)

Tarrytown

Overlooking the Hudson River, this Gothic
Revival-style house was designed in 1838
by Alexander Jackson Davis as a country villa
for former New York City Mayor William
Paulding. In 1864–1865, the mansion was
doubled in size for the second owner,
New York merchant George Merritt. In
1961, the 67-acre estate was donated to the
National Trust for Historic Preservation.
The stonework of our replica is made of
elm bark. The window casings are fabricated
with bamboo and salt cedar branches, while
the bay window details are composed of
shelf fungus, cinnamon curls, beech seeds,
gourd seeds, and juniper berries.

53

Sunnyside

Sunnyside (1835)

Tarrytown

This romantic house overlooking the Hudson
River was built by writer and diplomat
Washington Irving as a retreat after decades
of traveling abroad and exploring the American
West. Originally a simple 18th-century stone
cottage, Irving extensively enlarged and
remodeled it in the 1830s with the help of his
neighbor, George Harvey, a landscape painter.
The façade of our version is made of sand in
tinted grout. The roof, shutters, and door
are made of leaves. Twigs frame the windows
while cedrella pods provide the dormer
eave decoration.

Montgomery Place (1805)

Annandale-on-Hudson

Set amid more than 400 acres with views of the
Hudson River and the Catskill Mountains, this
Federal-style house was designed by Alexander
Jackson Davis. The open pavilion, with its high
arcade articulated by engaged Corinthian columns
that framed wide views of the river, is one of its
most impressive features. The railings on our
replica are made of screw pods and corkscrew hazel
branches. Willow, cinnamon, and poppy pods
form the windows, while the details are constructed
of birch bark, acorn tops, and pine cone scales.

Olana (1891)
Hudson

Olana, named for a fortress treasure-house in ancient Persia, was the home of Frederic Edwin Church, a major figure in the Hudson River School of landscape painting. Built between 1870 and 1891, it was inspired by the Moorish architecture Church saw on an extended trip to Europe and the Middle East. He disengaged Richard Morris Hunt, the designer of his first house on the property, and hired Calvert Vaux to design his new dream house. Our Olana has siding of horse chestnut bark and a roof of eucalyptus leaves. The ornamentation is made of pussy willow, alder cones, beech seeds and hulls, gourd seeds, burning bush twigs, lotus pods, star-anise, and willow sticks.

Kykuit (1913)
Pocantico Hills

Kykuit—Dutch for "lookout"—is a 40-room villa with breathtaking views of the Hudson River, built for oil tycoon John D. Rockefeller by the architectural firm of Delano & Aldrich. The classical revival mansion's interiors were designed by Ogden Codman, Jr. In 1979, the house, its furnishings, and 87 of the estate's 4,000 acres were donated by his grandson, then New York Governor Nelson Rockefeller, to the National Trust for Historic Preservation. Our mansion has a roof of magnolia leaves. The ironwork is composed of eucalyptus leaves, stems, and seed pods, juniper berries, hickory nut shells, and beech seed pods; pine bark forms the stonework. The figures are fashioned out of pistachio shells, honeysuckle vines, and wheat grain, and their hair is made of tree lichen, yarrow, and dusty miller. The eagle is constructed from willow leaves, ash seeds, and hickory nuts.

Covered Bridge (ca. 1870)

The covered wood bridges of New York State reflect the history and development of its communities and transportation systems. Beginning in the early 19th century, it became evident that protecting a bridge's structural system from the elements would reduce maintenance and replacement costs. This was achieved by covering the timber truss bridge with a roof and board sheathing to enclose the frame structure. Our bridge has cork bark walls, a red oak leaf roof with corkscrew hazel twigs on top.

Philipsburg Manor (1680)
Sleepy Hollow

The Philipse family was one of the wealthiest in New York in the 18th century and the Manor was the center of their commercial trade business. They were also among the largest slaveholders in the area and Loyalists in the Revolutionary War. As a result, the property was confiscated in 1779 and the family fled to England. Today Philipsburg Manor is a living history museum with a Manor House, gristmill, barns, and costumed interpreters. Our manor has elm bark for the stone walls, cattails for the upper siding, and a sycamore bark roof.

Overleaf
Van Cortlandt Manor (1748)
Croton-on-Hudson

This stone manor house is likely built on the foundation of an earlier fort trading post from around 1665. Situated at the confluence of the Croton and Hudson Rivers, the house was completed in 1748. The following year, Pierre Van Cortlandt, New York State's first lieutenant governor, moved there with his wife. The siding of our replica is made of cedar bark; the chimney details are fashioned out of honeysuckle, willow, and acorn tops. Pine bark is used to make the stone, and the shutters were crafted from redbud pods. The porch posts and rails are molded from winged euonymus, and the porch floor and stairs are cedar.

63

Published by Shop in the Garden Books
The New York Botanical Garden
Bronx, New York 10458
www.nybgShopintheGarden.org

Developed by Shop in the Garden Books:

Catherine Hipp
Associate Vice President, Garden Retail
and Business Development

Ellen Bruzelius
Director of Business Development

Produced in association with Patrick Filley Associa

Designed by Salsgiver Coveney Associates

Edited by Sally A. Leone and Margaret Falk

Special thanks to Director of Glasshouses
Francisca Coelho and the Enid A. Haupt Conservat
staff for their indispensable help in setting up and
maintaining the show each year.

Thanks also to LGB of America for use of their
train image on the endpapers.

Printed in Hong Kong

ISBN 0-89327-968-4

Proceeds from the sale of this book support
The New York Botanical Garden's pursuit of
excellence in horticulture, education, and science.